Coffee With Jesus

An Eight Week Morning Devotional

by Todd Uebele

i

Coffee With Jesus
By Todd Uebele
Third Edition

ISBN 13: 978-0-9831009-9-7
ISBN 10: 0-9831009-9-3

One Body Press
info@onebodypress.org

One Body Press
www.onebodypress.org
info@onebodypress.org

THIRD EDITION

What a privilege and an honor it is to me to have *Coffee With Jesus* published in its third edition!

I will grant, CWJ has never shown up on the New York Times bestseller list, or any best seller list for that matter. However, it has been running a steady race, helping people grow in their walk for over 15 years!

This edition provides some much needed updates to some of the anecdotes used illustrate the daily lessons. Some of the scriptures are updated as well. Finally, a few items that slipped through our editing process have been addressed.

Words cannot express my appreciation to all those who have supported me since the first version of this devotional has been run. It's been a long steady race and I look forward to running it even longer!

TABLE OF CONTENTS

ACKNOWLEDGEMENTS

There are several people with whom this would not have been possible. I would be remiss if I did not thank them and acknowledge the help, encouragement and support they have given me.

First and foremost is my wife, the key to my happiness. She has stood by me through some pretty rough storms and been a great support in my studies and in my writing.

The following people have provided me with a great deal of insight and encouragement as I plowed through the individual studies before putting a bunch together in a devotional book: Andrea for helping through one of the most difficult periods in my life, Al, for your mentoring and guidance. Yilda for being my sounding board and my friend.

PREFACE

Lord make me an instrument of your peace

Where there is hatred,
Let me sow love;
Where there is injury, pardon;
Where there is error, truth;
Where there is doubt, faith;
Where there is despair, hope;
Where there is darkness, light;
And where there is sadness, Joy.

O Divine Master grant that I may not so much seek to be consoled
As to console;
To be understood, as to understand;
To be loved, as to love.
For it is in giving that we receive,
It is in pardoning that we are pardoned,
And it is in dying that we are born to eternal life.

-- The Peace Prayer of St. Francis --

It is my prayer that in reading these devotions, you find yourself closer to our Father, more like His Son, and in tune with His Spirit.

TRU

Week 1: The Grace of God

Day One: Who Is Jesus?

Scripture: Isaiah, 9:6, Matthew 16:13-16

"At the name of Aslan, each one of the children felt something jump in his inside. Edmund felt a sensation of mysterious horror. Peter felt suddenly brave and adventurous. Susan felt as if some delicious smell or some delightful strain of music had just floated by her. And Lucy got the feeling you have when you wake up in the morning and realize that it is the beginning of the holidays or the beginning of summer."
- C.S. Lewis, The Lion, The Witch and the Wardrobe

Jesus Christ caused quite a stir in His day. During His life, and in all the centuries since, there has been a tremendous amount of debate over just who Jesus is and was. Many people back then did not know who Jesus was. He was someone different to different people. Today, many still do not know. As we begin our walk with Christ, I think it is important to start out by looking at exactly who He is.

The first portrayal of Jesus we have is as a man. He was "born of a woman" (Gal 4:4), and was a flesh and blood human being. Not only does the Bible show Jesus being born as flesh and blood, we can also see evidence of Jesus' humanity all throughout His ministry. Jesus Christ had hunger (Matthew 4:2), tiredness (Luke 8:23), anguish (Luke 22:44), and He faced temptation just like you and I (Matthew 4:1-11).

Everything that you have gone through, Jesus has gone through as well. He was fully human, and faced the same trials that we all face. He overcame them two ways: 1) Relying on the Word of God, "It is written: 'Man does not live on bread alone.'" (Luke 4:4), and 2) Submitting to the Will of God, "Father, if you are willing, take this cup from me; yet not my will, but yours be done." (Luke 22:42).

He was both loved by many and hated by many. Jesus was different things to different people, but He has touched, in some way, everyone on this planet. His teachings have probably had the single greatest impact on humanity. The question remains, though, who exactly was He? Who *is* He? Ask yourself, "Who is Jesus to me?"

Day Two: He's Alive!!!

Scripture: 1 Corinthians 15:12-22

"Christ is risen from the dead: arise with him. Christ returns to himself: you also must return to him. Christ has come forth from the tomb: free yourselves from the fetters of evil. The gates of hell are open and the power of death is destroyed. The old Adam is superseded, the new perfected. In Christ a new creation is coming to birth: renew yourselves. "
-- Gregory Nazianzen

1 Corinthians 15 is an absolutely awesome chapter. I love this chapter. I think this chapter says so much about the purpose of Christ, the purpose of Christianity, and the purpose of Christians. In this chapter, Paul "lays it on the line." I was reading it just the other day, when one verse jumped out at me.

In verses 12 through 19, Paul tells them, and us, that if Christ did was not raised from the dead, our faith is in vain and we are blasphemers. Seven times Paul mentions, "If not..." But if it is preached that Christ has been raised from the dead...If there is no resurrection ...if Christ has not been raised...in fact the dead are not raised...if the dead are not raised, then Christ has not been raised either...if Christ has not been raised...but then...then, the kicker, verse twenty:

> But Christ has indeed been raised from the dead, the first fruits of those who have fallen asleep.

But. Christ. has. indeed. been. raised. Christ has been raised!!! I almost get the feeling Paul set them up and then clinched them. Christ has indeed been raised from the dead. "No more sin's sting, no more suffering!" We are free from the bondage of sin because Jesus Christ died and was raised from the dead. "God made him who had no sin to be sin for us, so that in him we might become the righteousness of God" (2 Corinthians 5:21). He is alive and we are made alive through Him. What a blessing!!

Day Three: Conditional Grace?

Scriptures: Titus 3:4-7, Daniel 9:17-18, Romans 3:22-24; 6:23, Ephesians 1:5-6; 2:6-10

"When a person works an eight hour day and receives a fair day's pay for his time, that is a wage. When a person competes with an opponent and receives a trophy for his performance, that is a prize. When a person receives appropriate recognition for his long service or high achievements, that is an award. But when a person is not capable of earning a wage, can win no prize, and deserves no reward -- yet receives such anyway as a gift of love -- that is a good picture of God's grace."
-- Nita Johnson, World for Jesus Ministries

I came across something on the internet one day that really disturbed me. Somebody had written a book claiming that God's Grace was conditional. My first thought was *conditional grace is not grace*, but then I got thinking, "Is God's grace really conditional? What kind of conditions are there? How do I know I received His grace?" At one point, you too may have questioned whether or not you really received God's grace.

Well, if you have or are now having those questions, I have answer. An emphatic YES you have received God's grace, in full. I think one of the things Paul is most adamant about in his letters is that we cannot earn God's Grace. Our salvation comes from nothing we have done. God's grace is, in fact, *unmerited favor* bestowed by Him.

Not only is God's Grace unmerited and undeserved, but it is a gift of God that He gives freely to all who would receive His Son. The Bible tells us that Grace is free, it is a gift of God, it is available to all men, and it is, in fact, unmerited, undeserved favor bestowed upon us by God. It is once we accept His grace and love that we can fully begin to know the person of Jesus, His Father, and the Holy Spirit.

Does the Bible ever put conditions on God's Grace? NO! God loves us unconditionally with all our faults. In fact, the only reason we can love God and accept His Grace is because He loved us first, "While we were still sinners, Christ died for us" (Romans 5:8)

Day Four: Cleaned By God

Scriptures: Malachi 3:2, Hebrews 9:14

"There is no such thing as a once-for-all fullness. It is a continuous appropriation of a continuous supply from Jesus Christ. It is a moment by moment cleansing and a moment by moment filling. As I trust Him, He fills me. So long as I go on trusting Him, He goes on filling me. The moment I begin to believe, that moment I begin to receive. As long as I keep on believing, praise the Lord, I keep on receiving."
-- Charles Inward

When my son was little, he *loved* donuts (wonder where he got it from). In particular, he loves chocolate covered donuts. On Saturdays, it is a tradition of my family and I to go and get donuts. On one particular Saturday, he had his chocolate covered donut and as usual, he got more chocolate *on* his mouth than *in* his mouth. Before helping him out of the chair, I grabbed a wipey and went to clean him up. Man did he struggle! He squirmed and twisted and fought, it was not a pleasant experience for the little man. The thing is, he needed to be cleaned. If not his face would have been all sticky, it would have attracted dirt and germs and other unpleasantness. I was trying to help him, I knew what was better for him, but from his point of view, it was not a pleasant experience. It must have been close to torture! I did clean him though, and when all was said and done he was happy (he even said "tanku dad"), and he was much better off.

The experience made me stop and think. How many times has my Father tried to clean me? How many times have I fought against Him when he tries to clean me? When God cleans us, it is not always fun, it is not always pleasant, but He does know what is best for us. He is trying to clean us from things that lead to death.

While not a pleasant experience, God's cleaning leads to life. While, by nature we may squirm and twist in fight, in the end we will be much better off for having been cleaned. Then we too will say, "Tanku Dad."

Day Five: "I need HELP!"

Scriptures: Psalm 18:6, Isaiah 41:10, Hebrews 13:6

"I was embarrassed to be such a fool in a situation that I had told myself and other people countless times I would never submit to -- talking to a psychiatrist, ostensibly seeking help, but without any confidence that he could give it. I have never believed these people can do anything for an intelligent man he can't do for himself. I have known many people who leaned on psychiatrists, and every one of them was a leaner by nature, who would have leaned on a priest if he had lived in an age of faith, or leaned on a teacup reader or an astrologer if he had not enough money to afford the higher hokum."
-- Robertson Davies, The Manticore

My daughter used to *hate* cleaning her room. Every week, it was the same fight, and somehow, every week, despite being cleaned just six or seven days earlier, you needed a machete and native guide to cross her room. After one exhausting day, with very little cleaning done, I removed the TV from her room and told her she would not get it back until her room was clean.

Her response was desperate and immediate, "But *DAD*, I can't do it... I need HELP!" Normally when my daughter says she can't do something, it means she does not want to, however in this case, where heavy machinery might get the job done in the time allotted, I could see she really did need help.

Looking back, it made me think. *How many times have I said that very same thing to my Father? How many times have I cried to God, "I can't do it... I need HELP!"* When my family and I moved to Mississippi, we went through more than our share of trials. There were many days that I got on my knees crying to God asking Him for help.

My Father not only heard my prayers, He answered them. He provided the help and guidance and comfort I needed. Are you struggling? Do you need help? Ask God, he promises aid and He makes good on His promises. There is no problem too big or too small. If you can't do it, God can help.

Day Six: Our Savior

Scripture: Philippians 2:5-8, Hebrews 7:23-25, 1 John 4:14

"Then I was inspired. Now I'm sad and tired. After all, I've tried for three years. Seems like ninety. Why then am I scared to finish what I started... what you started? I didn't start it. God, thy will is hard. But you hold every card. I will drink your cup of poison. Kneel me to your cross and break me. Bleed me, beat me, kill me, take me now..."
-- Andrew Lloyd Weber, Jesus Christ Superstar

Not only was Jesus God, not only was Jesus man, but he voluntarily gave up His exalted position in Heaven to become man. What's more, he was so obedient that He voluntarily gave up his life on earth to death on a cross! That begs the question, "Why?" Why did Jesus Christ give up being God to become man and die on a tree?

The answer, quite simply, is to be our Savior. Jesus was born, just for the purpose of being our savior. Immediately after His birth, the angels told the shepherds, "Today, in the town of David, a Savior has been born to you. He is Christ, the Lord." (Luke 2:10). From the day of His birth, Jesus was destined to suffer and die on a wooden cross to take the penalty for our sins.

And suffer and die is just what Jesus did. Jesus died for you. He gave up everything on the cross for you. Then He rose for you! Now, He is our savior and, through Him, we may spend eternity with our Father, in Heaven. Today, let's say thank you to our savior, Jesus!

Day Seven: Why Do We Need God's Grace??

Scripture: Genesis 3:8, 22-24, Romans 3:21-24, 5:12-13, 1 Peter 2:24-25

"I had neither kith nor kin in England, and was therefore as free as air -- or as free as an income of eleven shillings and sixpence a day will permit a man to be. Under such circumstances, I naturally gravitated to London, that great cesspool into which all the loungers and idlers of the Empire are irresistibly drained."
-- "A Study in Scarlet", Sir Arthur Conan Doyle

This week, we learned about God's gift of grace. We saw how He cleans us, helps us and saves us through His Son. At this point, you may be thinking to yourself, *well, that is great that Jesus came to be the savior of the world and that God has given us the wonderful gift of grace, but why do I need His grace?* My friend, I thought you would never ask!

When God first created the world and created man, He was in fellowship with man. They walked together and talked together, but then man disobeyed God. He sinned and that sin separated him from God.

As a result of Adam and Eve's sin, we are all sinners. Sin came into the world through Adam, and as a result we are all sinners, but Jesus Christ came to saves us from our sins and from the death that is the result of our sin. God, by His grace can now justify us through our savior, Jesus Christ, because Jesus took our sins upon Himself and died in our place.

Jesus paid the penalty for our sin by dying on the cross. So, with Jesus dying in our place, we can now be restored to the Father through Him. Jesus died so that we may have life. Where Adam brought sin and death, Jesus brings forgiveness and life. That is why Jesus came from Heaven to Earth. That is why Jesus became man. That, my friend, is why Jesus died on the cross....so that by God's grace we may be restored through Him and have eternal life!

Week I Notes

Week II: Walk the Walk

Day One: Submitting to our Father

Scriptures: James 4:7, Romans 6:13-14, Matthew 26:39

"What you need to do, is to put your will over completely into the hands of your Lord, surrendering to Him the entire control of it. Say, "Yes, Lord, YES!" to everything, and trust Him to work in you to will, as to bring your whole wishes and affections into conformity with His own sweet, and lovable, and most lovely will. It is wonderful what miracles God works in wills that are utterly surrendered to Him."
-- Hannah Whitewall Smith, God of All Comfort

When my son was one, he absolutely hated having things on his head. Anything, hats, covers, hoods made him mad. He did not even like having a shirt go over his head. He would fight and struggle and fuss to no end. Eventually, when the fight was out of him, he would sit still and I would put his shirt on. It only took 10 seconds to do, but with him struggling, it usually lasted 4 or 5 minutes! Sometimes it would get frustrating. If he would only just not fight, it would be over before he knew it. There would be nothing to be afraid of. It would not even be an issue.

One day, after struggling to get his shirt on, I asked in frustration, "was that so bad??" Looking back on that moment, I wondered if God got frustrated with me. Too many times, he would try to take care of me, much like I would try and take care of my boy, and, much like him, I would fight and struggle and fuss to no end, only to give up and submit. Once I submitted, though, God's work was painless, and I was much better off.

There is a line in an old Rich Mullins song that goes, "I would rather fight you for something I don't really want than take what you give to me." Why do I fight God, when if I just submitted to Him things would be so much easier? When we submit ourselves to His will, life is often much smoother than when we fight it. So why do we fight?

My son has since learned not to fight with the shirt, indeed, now he even helps. Dressing him is so much easier when he submits to my will. When we submit ourselves to God, life will proceed much smoother. Are you fighting God? Why not try submitting to Him today?

Day Two: Baptism, The First Mark of Obedience

Scripture: Matthew 28:18-20, Mark 16:15-18, Galatians 3:26-29, Romans 6:1-5, 1 Peter 3:18-22, Colossians 2:11-15

"We can disobey God if we choose, and it will bring immediate relief to the situation, but we shall be a grief to our Lord. Whereas if we obey God, He will look after those who have been pressed into the consequences of our obedience. We have simply to obey and to leave all consequences with Him. Beware of the inclination to dictate to God as to what you will allow to happen if you obey Him."
-- Oswald Chambers, My Utmost for His Highest

What is baptism, and what is it for? Baptism is the first command to be obeyed by a Christian. Why the first command, and why is it so important? Indeed, why is it commanded by Jesus Himself? Well, baptism has dual significance. One: It symbolizes the death, burial and resurrection of Jesus Christ, and two: it symbolizes the inner change that takes place when we put all our hope and trust in our Lord Jesus Christ.

When Jesus Christ was to begin his public ministry, He was baptized by John the Baptist. When it ended, He was crucified, buried and raised to life. Those events changed the world, and made possible the gift of grace God has given us. Part of the reason for our baptism is to symbolize that which Jesus went through: His death, His burial, and His resurrection. By going through the ritual, you identify yourself more closely with the Lord who sacrificed His all for you, and you partake of the same immersion as Jesus.

Baptism is also a very public event. It is a profession of faith. It is your way of telling the rest of Christ's Church that you now belong, that you have trusted in God. You have appealed to God and placed your faith in His Son. Baptism is probably the most important command that a Christian will ever follow, which is why it is the very first command a Christian should follow. Have you been baptized yet? Was it explained to you? What did it mean to you?

Day Three: Show me the FAITH!

Scriptures: Hebrews 11:1-2, Titus 2:7-8, James 2:17-18

"To have faith is to rely upon Christ, the Person, with the whole heart. It is not the understanding of the mind, not the theological opinion, not creed, not organization, not ritual. It is the koinonia of the whole personality with God and Christ, ... This experience of communion with Christ is itself the continual attitude of dependence on the Saviour which we call faith."
-- Kokichi Kurosaki, One Body in Christ

Faith is a funny thing. Like patience, it doesn't come easily and it is earned/developed more than given. One develops faith through adversity, but even then it can be a funny thing. Faith is the most important thing to a Christian, next to love. Our faith is our foundation (1 Peter 2:4-6). It saves us (Romans 5:1-2), sustains us (1 Kings 17:13-16), rejuvenates us (Hebrews 4:1-5), and carries us when we cannot carry ourselves (2 Corinthians 1:8-11).

Evelyn Husband, the wife of the Columbia Shuttle Commander, Rick Husband, illustrates all these points very well. Since the death of her husband, Evelyn has been very outspoken about how God has carried her through her grief. In an interview printed in Today's Christian Woman, she said, "I can make it through this crisis because what I believed about God in my head now has proven true in my heart". What an example of faith!

She has made her faith a part of everything she is. We should make our faith a part of everything we are as well. As we grow in faith, we grow as Christians. Ironically as we grow as Christians, we also grow in faith! The Bible is full of promises concerning faith. It is also full of examples of how those promises are tried and true. Our faith must not be kept to ourselves. It should be shining and active. We need to act out in faith, so we can bring glory to God. Doing so helps Christians and non-Christians alike. Christians will see an example and see live proof of how God is true to His Word. Non-Christians will see God in our actions, and may "see the light," and be won over for the Kingdom. Our faith is an integral part of our lives, working with us and through us to help us grow and better serve our Father in Heaven.

Day Four: Repaint, Thin No More!

Scriptures: John 8:10-11, Romans 6:-13, 1 John 1:7-9

Evangelical repentance is repentance of sin as sin: not of this sin nor of that, but of the whole mass. We repent of the sin of our nature as well as the sin of our practice. We bemoan sin within us and without us. We repent of sin itself as being an insult to God. Anything short of this is a mere surface repentance, and not a repentance which reaches to the bottom of the mischief. Repentance of the evil act, and not of the evil heart, is like men pumping water out of a leaky vessel, but forgetting to stop the leak.
-- C.H. Spurgeon

The story is told of a man who tried to hoodwink the local church. The church was in desperate need of painting, and this man, who gave the lowest bid, thought to cheat them. He gave them an estimate based on hours and amount of paint to be use, but when it came to the actual job, he cut the latex based paint with thinner. Using only half the paint that would be needed, he planned on pocketing the money he saved. Just as he was finishing his last stroke, the sky darkened, and opened up. The rain came in from nowhere, completely washing away the man's work. It looked as if he had not painted a single stroke. Then, just as quickly as it started, the rain stopped. The clouds broke up and the sun came out. The man heard a loud voice booming from Heaven that said, "Repaint, repaint, thin no more!"

Many times, people try to cheat God. They like to take advantage of His wonderful gift of grace. They look at it as a license to sin. Some people feel that because we do not need to earn God's Grace that we can do whatever we please. That is not the case. God did not free us from the bondage of sin so that we could be free to return to it. The word "repent" literally means, "to turn away," and when we repent from sin, we should turn away from sin. God's Grace is a gift of love, not a sin license. Humans are not perfect. We are sinful beings by nature, and God forgives us when we confess our sins to Him. We must confess our sins to Him, though. Then, we must make every effort to "turn away" from our sin. Is there some sin that is hanging over you today? Confess it to God, let Him free you from it, then "go now and leave your life of sin."

Day Five: Love Your Neighbor

Scriptures: Matthew 22:34-40, Romans 13:8-10, John 15:12,17

"Every gun that is made, every warship launched, every rocket fired signifies in the final sense, a theft from those who hunger and are not fed, those who are cold and are not clothed. This world in arms is not spending money alone. It is spending the sweat of its laborers, the genius of its scientists, the hopes of its children. This is not a way of life at all in any true sense. Under the clouds of war, it is humanity hanging on a cross of iron."
-- Dwight D. Eisenhower

Jesus said that all the commandments could be summed up by loving God and loving your neighbor. By the words of the Word Himself, all the commandments are summed up by love. His Apostle, Paul, further clarifies under inspiration that love does not harm to its neighbor. That being so, he echoes Christ in saying, "love is the fulfillment of the law."

Not only is love fulfillment of the law, but it is in itself a command of God. It is the command of God. Love is, or at least should be, our defining quality. With love everything else falls into place, humility, faith, hope, unity, etc. The list goes on and on. Without love, we cannot claim to be Christians, for God is love. If you have no love, you have no God, but if you have God and you have love. Further, if you submit yourself to Him, you will reflect his love and others will see Him in you.

Love without action is empty love and a man without love is an empty man. We need to act out in love. That means we need to help those in need. That may seem generic, but that one simple statement is very important. We need to help those in need. When an opportunity arises, jump at it. Even if it seems like a small thing, it could have a great impact. If we have love, we will help those in need. It is a natural progression. Love marks us as God's, for God is love, so people will know we are Christians by the love we show in what we do.

Love is, indeed, the greatest thing.

Day Six: Forgiveness

Scripture: Matthew 6:14-15

"People who harbor anger often don't realize it, but they are poisoning their own lives. When we don't forgive, we're not hurting the other person. We're not hurting the person that did us wrong.   We're not hurting God. We are only hurting ourselves. Leave it to God. Live a life of forgiveness. God sees every wrong that is done to you. God sees every person that's ever hurt you. He's keeping the record, and Scripture says if you let go, and don't seek revenge yourself God will pay you back.   He'll not only pay you back, He'll pay you back in abundance."
-- Andrea Strickland

A few decades ago, several American companies authorized by the government attempted to bury toxic waste products underground. They filled large metal containers with chemical waste, sealed the drums tight, and buried them deep under the ground. They thought that was the end of it. Within a short time, however, many of the containers started to leak and the toxic waste started seeping to the surface, which caused all kinds of problems. In some areas it killed all the vegetation and contaminated the water supply. Near Niagara Falls, a huge number of people began dying of cancer and other debilitating diseases. What went wrong? They tried to bury something that was too toxic. It couldn't be contained. They thought they could bury it and be rid of it forever. What they didn't realize was that the materials they were trying to bury were so powerful the containers couldn't hold them.   None of us are strong enough to contain the toxicity in our lives. We need help from someone bigger and stronger than ourselves.   That is why we need to give that bitterness, resentment, and other contaminants to God.   Forgive the people that hurt you.   Get rid of all that poison. Don't let the root of bitterness grow deeper and continue to contaminate your life.

And remember, you are not forgiving for their sake; you are forgiving for your sake.   You are forgiving so that poison doesn't continue to contaminate your life. If you do things God's way, he will not only fight your battles for you, but in the end, you'll come out better off than you were before.

Day Seven: Walking the Walk

Scriptures: Titus 2:7-8, 1 Peter 3:14-16

*"I'm often tempted to think how I'd like to change the people around me —
my wife, my kids, my associates — the list is endless. But changing others is
not the place to start. The place to start is with changing me. The more time
I've spent with others who I'd like to improve or change, the more this
principle applies to me. Something I've been doing, or failing to do, has
contributed to their current behavior patterns. If I am going to change their
behavior, I will need to change my behavior. To change them, I need to
change me."*
-- Jim Clemmer, Growing the Distance

When I was in school, I had the honor of being a "Midshipman Officer" my
first class, or senior year. My position was that of a platoon commander,
which means I had other midshipmen, or students, under my command.
Part of my job was making sure they carried themselves as future officers
should. In order for me to expect that from them, I needed to carry
myself as a future officer should.

Being in a place of leadership was a mixed blessing. I had certain rights
and privileges, but I also had a lot of eyes on me. Both my superiors and
those junior to me watched me, some closer than others, but all watched
me and saw how I carried myself. Not only did I have to teach concepts of
honor, duty, and integrity, but I had also had to live them.

Living as a Christian is much the same. We, as Christians, have the right
and privilege to be called Children of God, Co-Heirs with Christ. However,
with those rights and privileges also comes responsibility. We not only
need to teach love and hope and faith, but we must live them as well. The
whole world is watching, just waiting for us to mess up. While we will all
fall at times, we must strive to live the life that God has called us to. We
must love our fellow man, we must obey God, and we must have faith.
We must, walk the walk.

Week II Notes

Week III: Knowing God

Day One: Understanding God's Word

Scriptures: John 14:26, 16:13, 1 Cor. 2:13

"Breath in me, O Holy Spirit, that my thoughts may all be holy. Act in me, O Holy Spirit, that my work, too, may be holy. Draw my heart, O Holy Spirit, that I love but what is holy. Strengthen me, O Holy Spirit, to defend all that is holy. Guard me, then, O Holy Spirit, that I always may be holy."
-- Augustine

The Bible says that God's ways are so far above us, "as high as the heavens are above the earth", but just how high are the heavens above the earth? Let's be conservative and go with our nearest neighbor, Alpha Centauri. Alpha Centauri is 4.5 light years from earth. That is approximately 6,044,400,000,000 miles away. If it were possible to get in your car and drive, it would take 11,500,000 years to get there! Even if we take our fastest aircraft or missile, which goes about Mach 5 (five time the speed of sound), it would take 212,308 years! If we were to launch a mission today, our ancestors who arrive would be our great, great, great, great, great, great (plus 6,060 more "greats") grand children!

Does this sound mind boggling? I have to be honest, I am having trouble keeping up even as I am writing this, and that is with our *closest* star. Imagine if we use Sirius (the dog start) or Betelgeuse (in the constellation Orion)!

Understanding God's Word can be just as mind boggling. It is impossible to do on our own. Fortunately for us, God does not make us do it on our own. He gives us His Spirit. The Holy Spirit guides us, counsels us, and teaches us. When we rely on the Holy Spirit, we can know and understand God's Word. The mind gets "unboggled." When you read God's Word, pray and ask for Him to send His Spirit to guide you. He will send His Spirit and open your heart and mind to His glorious truth!

Day Two: Talking to God

Scripture: Genesis 4:26, Luke 11:1-13

To be used of God. Is there anything more encouraging, more fulfilling? Perhaps not, but there is something more basic: to meet with God. To linger in His presence, to shut out the noise of the city and, in quietness, give Him the praise He deserves. Before we engage ourselves in His work, let's meet Him in His Word . . . in prayer . . . in worship.
-- Charles (Chuck) R. Swindoll, "Insight for Living"

The day my son, Gabriel, returned from the hospital, I had a very large stack of jobs that needed to be accomplished. There was three days of mail and bills to go through, a mountain of laundry that needed to be folded and put away, more that needed to be washed, a kitchen of dishes to put away, not to mention feeding three kids and taking care of the youngest and his momma. I felt swamped!

When my oldest daughter returned from Girl Scouts, I heated up some dinner for her and sat down at the table with her. She looked at me and said, "Dad, would you like to talk, just you and me?" My heart melted. Suddenly I had absolutely nothing to do. My scheduled cleared and I had a lovely conversation with my daughter.

In the same way, God is awfully busy. He has six *billion* people to take care of, there are wars going on all over the world, earthquakes, diseases, He is a pretty busy guy. However, when we go to Him and say, "God, would you like to talk, just you and me?" His schedule clears. God *always* has time for us to talk to Him and it fills His heart with joy when we do. Have you talked to your Father yet today?

Day Three: Giving to God

Scriptures: 1 Cor. 16:1-3, 2 Cor. 9:12-13, 11:7-9, Malachi 3:8-11

"The purpose of tithing is to secure not the tithe but the tither, not the gift but the giver, not the possession but the possessor, not your money but you for God."
-- Anonymous

Why does God ask us to give back to Him? Surely He does not need our money? Well, we give not support God, but His Son's Church. Not just your local congregation, but the Church as a whole. Your tithes and offerings can be used to help support other congregations or missionaries. Paul collected offerings in Corinth and Galatia to help the Christians in Jerusalem. Did Paul literally steal money from the other churches? No, but those churches did support Paul in his ministry, and Paul did spread the Gospel all over the known world. When we give to God, we are helping spread His Word throughout the world by supporting His servants. Not only that, but giving itself can be a form of missions work. When we give to the needy, to those who cannot provide for themselves, we are fulfilling Christ's command to help the poor and needy, but even more; it presents an opportunity to bring those people into our family. By showing love and care, and doing an example of what is right, we can show people the love of God first hand.

There is more to it than that though. The command to give is one that comes with a promise. When we give to God, He blesses us. The more freely and happily we give, the more we get blessed. This is a promise I can personally attest to. At the time of this writing, I had increased my tithe to support my church's missions program. Right after doing so, I got a promotion/raise at work, had an opportunity to work for paid overtime (being on salary, that is unusual), found a sizable check that I had thought was lost in the U.S. postal system, and received a full refund check from the local college. If you give to God freely and with cheerfulness of heart, He *will* bless you. Why not try it? Why not ask God how much He wants you to give, and then do so faithfully?

Day Four: Giving YOURSELF to God

Scripture: Philippians 2:5, 8, Ephesians 4:11-13, Titus 2:7-8

Worship is giving God the best that He has given you. Be careful what you do with the best you have. Whenever you get a blessing from God, give it back to Him as a love gift. Take time to meditate before God and offer the blessing back to Him in a deliberate act of worship. If you hoard a thing for yourself, it will turn into spiritual dry rot, as the manna did when it was hoarded. God will never let you hold a spiritual thing for yourself; it has to be given back to Him that He may make it a blessing to others.
-- Oswald Chambers, My Utmost for His Highest

In the Old Testament, the Israelites were told to tithe from their flocks and their farms, in the New Testament, we are told to give monetarily. In both instances we are to give from our earnings, but is giving from our earnings really enough though? Is ten percent really enough? Is that all God wants, or as followers of Him, should we give more? Jesus Christ gave his all, literally. He gave 100% of who He was, not 10% of what he earned, or what He had, but 100%! He gave up the glory of Heaven to become a man, and then he gave up his life as a man...to death on a cross! We should follow his example, by giving ourselves 100% to God. We should dedicate, not only all we *have* to the Lord, but all that we are!

The Lord wants us to give from ourselves and of ourselves. He wants us give everything we are, both in service and in love. But how do we do this, you ask? The Lord has given us each our own gifts. God has given us all gifts to use in service to Him. Each of us has different gifts, but each of us has gifts of our own. If you are unsure as to what your gifts are, you can serve God just by living right. This goes back to following Christ's example. If we do our best to live like He does, then people will notice the difference. They will see the way you live, the way you are, and that gives you an opening to witness to them.

How are you living? How do you act in your workplace? How do you act when no one is watching? What kind of life do you live outside of church? Do people see God when they look at you?

Day Five: The Teaching of Christ, I

Scriptures: John 1:1-3, John 7:16-18, Hebrews 1:1-3

"A chasm is opening between the men who believe their Bibles and the men who are prepared for an advance upon Scripture. Inspiration and speculation cannot long abide in peace. Compromise there can be none. We cannot hold the inspiration of the Word, and yet reject it; we cannot believe in the atonement and deny it; we cannot hold the doctrine of the fall and yet talk of the evolution of spiritual life from human nature; we cannot recognize the punishment of the impenitent and yet indulge the 'larger hope.' One way or the other we must go. Decision is the virtue of the hour."
-- C. H. Spurgeon

What exactly is the "Teaching of Christ" that John is referring too? Some teach that the teachings of Christ consist of Matthew through Revelation only, and that Genesis through Malachi does not apply. However, according to the Bible, *all* scripture is God breathed, and is useful for teaching, rebuking, correcting and training in righteousness" (2 Timothy 3:16). If one is going to refer to part of the Bible as the teaching of Christ, he really should refer to all of it. Genesis through Malachi should be included in this, not discarded.

Jesus is the Word. He was with God; He is God. His teachings have come to us since the very beginning: through Moses, the prophets and then through Jesus Himself. EVERYTHING that is in God's Word has come from Jesus. It is true that in the Old Testament Christ did not physically teach the Israelites through the prophets, but rather the teaching came from God. Some argue that was God the Father, and not Christ. By Christ's own words though, He and the Father are one (John 10:30).

Jesus testified to His own teaching, and He testified that He received His teaching from the Father. The teaching of Christ was really the teaching of God, just like Moses and the prophets. Jesus was much greater, though, in that He Himself is God. So the teaching of God is also the teaching of Christ. Jesus is the Word, so we see that all the Word is, well, from the Word. Jesus *is* the Word, so everything the Bible teaches us, from Genesis to Revelation, is the Teaching of Christ.

Day Six: The Teaching of Christ, II

Scriptures: 2 John (1):7-10, 1 John 2:20-23

What I believe is so magnificent, so glorious, that it is beyond finite comprehension. To believe that the universe was created by a purposeful, benign Creator is one thing. To believe that this Creator took on human vesture, accepted death and mortality, was tempted, betrayed, broken, and all for love of us, defies reason. It is so wild that it terrifies some Christians who try to dogmatize their fear by lashing out at other Christians, because tidy Christianity with all answers given is easier than one which reaches out to the wild wonder of God's love, a love we don't even have to earn.
-- Madeleine L 'Engle

Yesterday, we saw that the Teaching of Christ includes the whole of Scripture. What we really saw, though, is the teaching *from* Christ. What if, the teaching *of* Christ meant the teaching *about* Christ? There are many, many passages in the Bible that can be looked at in two different ways, and this is one of them. However, this is one of those rare passages where both ways of looking at it could be not only correct, but complimenting each other.

In the first part of the passage from 2 John, he tells us that that some people have denied certain teachings about Jesus. They denied he came in the flesh. This was part of Gnosticism, which was a heresy that was running rampant at the time John was writing that letter.

Immediately after that passage that John tells us, "Anyone who runs ahead and does not continue in the teaching of Christ does not have God." It is very likely by what he was saying, that the teaching of Christ could be the teaching about Christ in this case. In his first letter, John tells us, "No one who denies the Son has the Father" (1 John 2:22), which matches what he says in 2 John (1):9. Isn't great how The Word is consistent in its teachings?

Day Seven: Reflecting God

Scriptures: Daniel 12:3, Matthew 5:14-16, 2 Cor. 3:17-18

"It is possible to shine as one of God's stars against the atmosphere of Satan's kingdom. In eternity "we shall shine as stars forever" as chandeliers of love, as God's eternal mood reflecting the Son's grace. If a person has areas of dishonesty or weakness, he must overcome them by living by every Word of God, by deliberately being set apart, and by walking in the filling of the Holy Spirit."
-- Carl Stevens, Invest in Doctrine

Whether you realize it or not, the moon as a tremendous impact on our lives. Tides, seasons, even our calendars are all determined by the moon. It gives us light to help us at night, sometimes nearly as bright as the sun during the day. It can light our path and help us find our way in the dark.

But what is the moon? People used to say green cheese, but over 30 years ago, man walked on the moon and we found out that the moon itself was just a dead rock. It's a big dead rock, but still a dead rock. It is lifeless, completely unable to do anything on its own. However, when it reflects the sun, it gives us light to see by and to guide us.

In the same way, we need to reflect the Son. Without Jesus, we are dead and lifeless. We cannot help people all by ourselves. However, when we reflect the Son, we can be a light to people in the dark. We can guide them and help them find their way when they are lost. With the Son, we can have a tremendous impact on people's lives.

The best way to reflect the Son is to constantly submit yourself to the Father. By talking to God, reading and understand His word and completely giving ourselves to Him, we will set a good example for Christians and non-Christians alike. The Bible tells us to let our light shine before *all* men, and we can only do that if we reflect God's Son. We, in essence, need to be moons. Ask yourself today, am I a moon?

Week III Notes

Week IV: Growing In Your Walk

Day One: Heavenly Wisdom

Scriptures: 1 Cor. 3:18-20, James 1:5-6, 3:13-17

"Let the first act on waking be to place yourself, your heart, mind, faculties, your whole being, in God's hands. Ask Him to take entire possession of you, to be the Guide of your soul, your Life, your Wisdom, your Strength. He wills that we seek him in all our needs, that we may both know Him truly, and draw closer and closer to Him; and in prayer we gain an invisible force which will triumph over seemingly hopeless difficulties."
-- Sidney Lear

"There is a way that seems right to a man, but in the end it leads to death," (Proverbs 14:12). That is a small, simple verse and yet so profound. So many people these days seek their own wisdom. They seek to be wise in the eyes of man and lift themselves up. The Lord has promised to send us His Spirit, and with Him, Heavenly Wisdom. Instead of seeking our own wisdom, we should submit ourselves to God and ask to be filled with His Wisdom.

The wisest earthly wisdom is foolishness to God. Without God's wisdom, we are all fools. We cannot serve God on our own. We cannot bring people to Him on our own. Stephen, one of the first deacons of the Church, amazed the people, not with his own wisdom, but with God's wisdom. He was full of the Spirit and full of Heavenly Wisdom, and because of this, did great things for God.

Ask our Father for Heavenly Wisdom. Submit yourself to Him and let Him fill you. There will not be an instant difference, but if you are faithful in asking for it, He is faithful in providing it.

Day Two: Unity

Scriptures: 1 Cor. 1:10, Philippians 1:27, 2:1-4, 1 Peter 3:8

"On the night of our Lord's betrayal and arrest He prayed that His people might be united. He suffered and died on the cross to break down the barriers of division, to put to death enmity and strife, to bring peace, and to reconcile all men 'in one body to God through the cross'. Jesus died in order to create a unified body of believers!!"
-- Al Maxey, Reflections #55

Unity for God's People is a noble, if not lofty goal. Jesus prayed for it, Paul encouraged, even stressed it. Yet today we see divisions over all kinds of doctrines. Our Lord and Savior, Jesus Christ wants unity in His people. He called for it, He prayed for it, and when He was still with His disciples, he warned them, "Every kingdom divided against itself will be ruined, and every city or household divided against itself will not stand" (Matthew 12:25).

The enemy seeks to divide the church, and to some extant has divided the church. In order to combat this, we must heed the calls of unity by Paul and Peter. If we do and if we can show love to our brothers and sisters, we can unite as a church and stand firm on the truth of Jesus Christ. For it is in Christ that we are unified (Romans 12:5). If we can make a stand together, we can be united in Christ.

The fact is, we can truly be united in Christ, and we can stand on the truth. We will not be popular, but our Lord and Savior was not even accepted by His own people. We should let tolerance overcome unity, we should not forsake our savior or dilute the truth for the sake of unity, but we should show love, patience and understanding. We should emulate our Lord.

We can do so by submitting to Him. Then, He will give us a spirit of unity among ourselves, so that with one heart and mouth we may glorify the God and Father of our Lord Jesus Christ.

Day Three: Maturity

Scriptures: 1 Cor. 14:20, Hebrews 5:13-14, 2 Timothy 3:14-17

"The knowledge of Christ's love for us should cause us to love Him in such a way that it is demonstrated in our attitude, conduct, and commitment to serve God. Spiritual maturity is marked by spiritual knowledge being put into action."
-- Edward Bedore, Berean Bible Institute

Yesterday, we saw how important unity of God's people is. In order to stand together and build up the church as a whole, we must first work on ourselves. We must grow in our spiritual maturity. Spiritual maturity is something we, as God's Children, should always be moving towards. The best way to grow in our thinking and in our maturity is by reading, praying over, and studying God's Word.

Not only do we need to study it, but we need to live it. We should always keep God's Word on our hearts. Not only reading it, but applying it. Maturity is not something that comes over night. It comes with years of spending time with alone with our Father, reading, studying, and *applying* His Word. Only when we make that our goal, and then follow that goal, can we mature as Christians.

As we become spiritually mature, it will be easier for us to discern what is from God and what is from the enemy. We will be able to detect false teachings and heresies that creep in and contribute to the moral ambiguity in the Church. Also, as we grow in maturity, it will be easier for us to overcome our pride, and as we grow as individuals, the church grows as a whole.

Day Four: Humility

Scriptures: Micah 6:8, Romans 12:3, 2 Timothy 2:23-24, James 4:10

"I have learned that much of my spiritual progress does not come directly from God, but through my ability to humble myself and hear Him speak through imperfect people. In fact, I have discovered that it pleases Him to hide His manifold wisdom in a variety of people and denominational perspectives. I know that the more I humble myself to others, the broader my understanding of God has actually become."
-- Francis Frangipane, "Ministries of Francis Frangipane"

One of the biggest obstacles to unity of God's people and to our own spiritual maturity is Pride. People say they separate over matters of worship and doctrine, but what is behind that? A person's pride. They are too proud to see that they could be misunderstanding or misinterpreting something. Their pride has them thinking that they are correct and everyone else is wrong. Unfortunately this sort of pride is running rampant in the church today.

Instead of joining the fray, we should set an example for the rest of the church. We need to be careful not let ourselves be drawn into foolish arguments. People will try to bait us, sure, but we must stay away. We should try to raise ourselves above the need to be right. We should ALWAYS defend the truth, and stand on the Truth, Jesus Christ, but this can be done better by living like Jesus and by being humble before the Church, then by getting involved in foolish arguments. If we reflect Jesus in our actions, we can have a much greater impact.

We can, and should, overcome our pride by being humble. Instead of getting involved in foolish arguments, we should reflect Jesus. When we *live* the truth, we will have a much greater impact on people. We must be humble, before God and before man. We should serve others, and raise them above ourselves. By putting aside our own interests and looking to those of others, we can reflect Jesus. Then the pride and folly of those who sow division and strife in the church will be exposed. "When pride comes, then comes disgrace, but with humility comes wisdom" (Proverbs 11:2).

Day Five: Hope

Scriptures: Philippians 3:12-14, Titus 2:11-14, Hebrews 6:18-20

"The best we can hope for in this life is a knothole peek at the shining realities ahead. Yet a glimpse is enough. It's enough to convince our hearts that whatever sufferings and sorrows currently assail us aren't worthy of comparison to that which waits over the horizon."
-- Joni Eareckson Tada

W. Colin McKay wrote a play entitled, "Hope Springs Eternal", where a teacher talks a lady out of jumping off a bridge, who, in turn talks the teacher out of jumping off that same bridge. One of the things the teacher tells the lady is that life is hope and that hope is eternal. As Christians we have hope in life and hope of being eternal.

Life is hard, everyone faces difficulties, but life on Earth is temporary. As Christians, we have the hope of eternal life with our Lord and Savior, Jesus Christ. That is a guaranteed hope. Nothing can take that away from you. Instead of focusing so much on the here and now, we should make the hereafter our focus. That is where the hope is. Everything here will pass away, but Jesus, He is eternal, and with Him in your life, you will be eternal as well.

Why not give up your earthly cares to our Father and hold on to the hope of eternal life we have in Christ Jesus.

Day Six: Endurance

Scriptures: Philippians 3:12-15, 1 Timothy 6:11-16, Revelation 3:21-22

"We in our turn have an assured confidence that we shall be able to leave this heritage unwaisted and enlarged to our children and our children's children. To do so we must show, not merely in great crises, but in the everyday affairs of life, the qualities of practical intelligence, of courage, of hardihood, and endurance, and above all the power of devotion to a lofty ideal, which made great the men who founded this Republic in the days of Washington, which made great the men who preserved this Republic in the days of Abraham Lincoln."
-- Theodore Roosevelt, Inaugural Address, 1905

Life itself can be quite hard, but it can be even more so, when there is another little life inside you. Seeing my wife go through two pregnancies, all I can do is sympathize with her, but I do give a great deal of sympathy. I also give her a great deal of credit. Being pregnant is not always fun. There is so much more to deal with: all sorts of stomach problems, sickness, gas, forgetfulness, not being able to tie your own shoes or bend over, the list goes on and on about all the indecencies a woman must go through while that little tiny human is growing inside her.

As if that were not bad enough, while pregnant, there are all sorts of things a woman must give up: alcohol, caffeine, artificial sweeteners. Then there are activities they can no longer do: skiing, skating, some even have to give up working! No, it is definitely not fun. However, when women endure all the indignities, and give up all the "fun stuff" they used to do, and make it to the birth of their child, the joy and elation they feel with the new life in their arms is unmatched, it is something men can only imagine, and then, barely.

Being a Christian is very similar to being pregnant. We have to put up with all sorts of indignities and persecutions from the world, and there is a lot of "fun stuff" that we must give up in our new life. However, if we can endure as Christians, to the very end, we will receive a new life. The joy and elation at meeting our Father and our Savior, and then spending eternity with them, will be something that is truly unmatched.

Day Seven: Christlikeness

Scriptures: Romans 8:28-29, John 13:13-15, Philippians 2:5-8, 3:20-21

"We are at this moment as close to God as we really choose to be. True, there are times when we would like to know a deeper intimacy, but when it comes to the point, we are not prepared to pay the price involved."
-- J. Oswald Saunders

Being like Christ is God's ultimate goal for each and every Christian. It should also be the goal *of* each and every Christian. "Whoever claims to live in him must walk as Jesus did." (1 John 2:6). It is what we should strive for each day of our lives. The decision though, can be costly.

We must choose to surrender our will to our Father, but what's more, we must do that constantly. Not only that, but if we want to be like Jesus, we must choose like He did when facing temptation. We simply must choose not to do what we should not. That is much easier said than done, and can prove to be costly. Paul lost a lot of respect and a lot of friends when he submitted to God, but he counted all that loss as gain, and we should too.

Part of being like Jesus, is making the same choices and decisions that He did. Christ was our example, and we should follow that example as best we can. If we can emulate Christ, if we can serve others, be humble, and grow closer to our Father, imagine how easy it will be for us as individuals to be united as a body of believers! Through maturity, humility and endurance, and by submitting to our Father daily, we truly can be like Christ and grow close to our Father in Heaven.

Week IV Notes

Week V: Growing Closer to God

Day One: Spring Cleaning

Scriptures: 1 John 1:6-10

"It is not necessary that every single member of the body should become useless and weak before death occurs. A weakness of, or a blow upon, the heart or the brain will suffice to bring an end to life, however strong and healthy other parts of the body may be. Thus one sin by its poisonous effect on the mind and heart is sufficient to ruin the spiritual life not of one only, but of a whole family or nation, even of the whole race. "
-- Sadhu Sundar Singh

When we moved into our first house, our "office" doubled as a closet, with coats and out of season clothes. We had some metal shelving that worked well as a hanging rod as well. We hung our coats and heavy clothes from the top shelf, which made the middle shelf useless. Unfortunately, the light was right above the shelving, so the coats blocked some of the light and the office seemed dimmer as a result. This arrangement lasted for about a year. During that time, the middle shelf made a good "hiding place." Whenever we needed to do some quick cleaning for company, or we did not know where to put something, the shelf was the perfect spot. Things seemed to just disappear. All throughout the year we put stuff there, hid it, and forgot about it.

The time finally came where we decided to make it an honest to goodness office, to use the room to its full potential. All the coats and all the clothing were relocated, and the office was a brand new room! It was more open, and much brighter. The light was allowed to permeate the entire space and it looked like a completely different room. However the light exposed all the "stuff" we had hidden away over the year. Every paper, every scrap was now out there for all to see. Many times there are things in our own life that keep us from our full potential. We each have our own "stuff" that we wish to hide and put up our own blockers. However, when we do that, the light of our Father cannot fully shine in us. We become dark and crowded. This spring, let us all do a little inner spring cleaning. Give up whatever you have blocking your "stuff" to the Father and let Him clean you. Then you will be a new creation. The Lord will be able to use you to your full potential, and His light will shine through!

Day Two: In My Father's Arms

Scriptures: Psalm 91:1-4

"Jesus was a rough and burly man. Full of fire and passion. A warrior when it came to doing battle against those who offended the sacred things of the Father. Yet, in a moment, able to touch a young child with hands of gentleness. To us the warrior is just as critical as the gentle shepherd. By His holy passion for righteous we are continually moved on to perfection. By His gentle love we are continually comforted in our lessons of life."
-- Daily Glory Devotions

One evening, soon after my youngest was born, I closed myself in my office to do my quiet time. As I started, I heard my baby whining from his crib. He typically whines a little bit and goes back to sleep around this time every evening, so I thought nothing of it and tried to start my praying. I had a lot to pray about...family issues, financial issues, etc. Once again everything seemed to be happening at once. I confess to being a little annoyed when the typical whine grew into full crying. I got up and went into his room, and picked him out of his crib. I tried changing his diapy; he cried. I tried giving him a bobba; he cried. I went through the "checklist" most fathers are given well after the fact; he cried.

Finally, I picked him up in my arms, sat in the rocking chair and sang to him while rocking back and forth. The crying went down to a whimper, then to a whine, then it stopped all together. He shuffled a little bit to get comfortable, then put his head down on my chest, curled his knees underneath him and closed his eyes and listened to my voice as my arms were wrapped around him.

It was definitely one of those "moments," but I didn't quite get it. I apologized to God for not being able to spend time with Him at that moment, and He said, "But you are." Then I realized...as I was sitting there, holding my baby boy in my arm, rocking and comforting him. My Father was holding me in His Arms, rocking me and comforting me. My problems were not instantly solved, but for that one moment, they had melted away: I was safe and secure in my Father's Arms.

Day Three: The Power of Prayer

Scriptures: Matthew 18:18-20; Philippians 4:4-7

"The spirit of prayer is a pressing forth of the soul out of this earthly life, it is a stretching with all its desire after the life of God, it is a leaving, as far as it can, all its own spirit, to receive a spirit from above, to be one life, one love, one spirit with Christ in God. For the love which God bears to the soul, His eternal, never-ceasing desire to enter into it, and to dwell in it, stays no longer than till the door of the heart opens for Him."
-- William Law

During a very active hurricane season, we evacuated all the way up to Nashville, TN for one of the storms. While we were in Nashville, we visited the Opry Plaza, a HUGE sprawling place, with a gigantic mall. As we were leaving the mall, I reached into my pocket and realized that my car keys were missing. I about died. Thoughts of being stranded at the mall 500 miles from home immediately came to mind...followed by each of the National Lampoon vacation movies.

We returned to the mall, and my wife sat with the kids as I back tracked all the stores we had gone to asking if anyone had turned in car keys. Each of them said "no." I was praying the whole entire time, but it wasn't until I went to the second to last store, which was the Bible Outlet store, that I knew I would find them. After helping me look for the keys in the store, I asked the clerk to pray for me. I knew I would find them then. After the last store, I went to the information booth, and the gentleman there told me that someone had, in fact, found a set of car keys to my model car and they had turned them into security. I half-ran to the security office and sure enough, they were sitting right there on the desk. God had answered my prayer and performed a miracle.

The probability of finding something as small as a set of car keys in a place that large is astronomical. The fact that those keys were found at all, let alone turned in is nothing short of a miracle, and I believe it was because two of us were in agreement in prayer. Prayer is powerful, powerful enough to find a set of keys in a place as huge as Opry Plaza in Nashville, TN.

Day Four: God's Timing

Scriptures: Romans 8:27-30; Luke 12:22-34

"God has wisely kept us in the dark concerning future events and reserved for himself the knowledge of them, that he may train us up in a dependence upon himself and a continued readiness for every event."
-- Matthew Henry

One morning, when my oldest son was still a toddler, I finally made my way out of bed and went downstairs. My wife was getting my son some cereal for breakfast. As she was getting ready to put him in his chair he said, "Come oooon, ma, come ooon"....

Apparently, she was not moving fast enough for the little man. He woke up hungry and wanted his fruit loops NOW!   Her first reaction was shock, that was not typical of Evan, but then she told him he'd get them when he got them.

I personally thought the episode was amusing, and so did she once the boy was settled in his seat. Looking back though, I cannot help but wonder how often I do that to my Father. How many times do I say, "Come oooon, God, come oooon", as I demand what I want NOW.

While He is not shocked at us, God does have the same reaction, doing things according to His timing. Solomon tells us, "He has made everything beautiful in its time." (Ecclesiastes 3:11), yet too often I try to set my own time table.

We know that, "in all things God works for the good of those who love him" (Rom 8:28), so why not try leaving the timing to Him and trust that he has our best interests in mind, even when we wake up hungry.

Day Five: A Strong Tower

Scriptures: Psalm 18:10; 61:3; 91:2-4

"In the secret of God's tabernacle no enemy can find us, and no troubles can reach us. The pride of man and the strife of tongues find no entrance into the pavilion of God. The secret of his presence is a more secure refuge than a thousand Gibraltars. I do not mean that no trials come. They may come in abundance, but they cannot penetrate into the sanctuary of the soul, and we may dwell in perfect peace even in the midst of life fiercest storms."
-- Hannah Whitall Smith

When my children were little, my wife would often get each of them something from the dollar section of Target. On one particular trip, my son's choice was a set of erasers. These were no ordinary erasers, they were sports erasers. Each one shaped like a different kind of ball. There were baseballs, basketballs, soccer balls, even footballs. My son does not need to do any erasing, mind you, but he loved the way they looked. Plus, they were only a dollar, a small price to pay for child to behave while you are doing your shopping. Later that evening my son and I were watching some shows together and he took out his erasers. He used them to build a nice tower on our coffee table. After he was done he looked at me and smiled. Not able to control myself, I grabbed the bottom one and pulled. He thought it was the funnies thing! I had never heard him laugh so loud! He promptly rebuilt the tower and said, "do it again, dad!"

We went back and forth a little bit, he would build the tower and I would knock it down. He was laughing so hard he was in tears. He wandered off after a little while only to return a few minutes later and rebuild his "tower" again. This time, I leaned over and blew real hard… and down came the tower! Again, my son went into hysterics. It was good fun for him, and easy for me. A tower of erasers is not that strong of a tower and very easy to knock down. In contrast, Christians have a tower that is stronger than anything we could ever imagine. The Bible says, "The name of the LORD is a strong tower; the righteous run to it and are safe" (Psalm 18:10). If you find yourself in adversity, hideout in the Lord, "under his wings you will find refuge; his faithfulness will be your shield and rampart" (Psalm 91:4b).

Day Six: How Wretched Am I!

Scripture: Romans 7:14-25

"Time and again God condemns the various lusts of the flesh, especially those that involve sexual immorality and the breaking of covenantal unions .... and time and again mankind shuns this divine guidance and wallows in the mire of his baser instincts, all to his own shame and harm. It seems sometimes that we never learn; that we are in a losing battle within ... torn between right and wrong, good and evil, the Spirit and the flesh."
-- Al Maxey, Reflections #107

At certain points in his life, Paul was a wretched man. He knew what was right and what was wrong, but he seemed to not do what was right and do what was wrong. Things are no different with people today. Man sins, man is full of sin. It hurts God when we sin, and it hurts us when we sin. So why do we do it?

The answer is we are born slaves to sin. Slaves to the flesh. We are doomed to a life of sin and separation. It seems just a little hopeless, no? That is why we are wretched people.

However, there is hope. While we will never be completely free from sin, we can break free of the chains that bind us. How? Look at Romans 7, verse 25: Through Jesus Christ our Lord! Through Jesus we can be free of sin. Free of the wretchedness that binds us. When we willingly submit ourselves to Him, we free ourselves from the snares of sin.

As you spend your time with the Lord this week, submit yourself Him daily. It is hard at first, but as we grow closer to Him, it gets easier. Have you submitted yourself to the Lord?

Day Seven: The Peace That Passes Understanding

Scriptures: Philippians 4:4-7; John 16:33; Isaiah 66:12-13

"If our minds are stayed upon God, His peace will rule the affairs entertained by our minds. If, on the other hand, we allow our minds to dwell on the cares of this world, God's peace will be far from our thoughts."
-- Woodroll Kroll

When I was a kid in Sunday School, one of my favorite songs was, "I've Got the Joy" (*I've got the joy, joy, joy, joy, down in my heart, to stay*). My favorite verse went like this: *I have the peace that passes understanding Down In My Heart*. As a kid, I really did not understand what it meant, but for some reason, I always liked singing that part. It was not until I got older and started going through the travails of high school, later college, and then (gasp) the "real world," that I truly understood the peace that passes understanding. It is a peace that allows perfect calm in the middle of life's storms, a peace that doesn't come from friends, family, or counselors (though all are good sources when going through rough times), but rather a peace that can only come from God himself. It is a peace He promises us, and a peace that, no matter what you are going through in life, can be yours.

Jesus promises us peace and rest when we rely on him. In the midst of life's storms and battles, He can and will provide us the comfort and courage we need to carry on. David and Paul both relied on the Lord and survived some pretty tough situations. They both reached the very bottom depths of despair, but found hope and peace in God. That same hope, that same peace, is available to us. All we need to do is cast our burdens upon the Lord. In the same way, we should be ready and willing to take each other's burdens. By putting the interests of others above those of ourselves, we can be instruments of the Lord's peace. Likewise, if you need to reach out, if you are in need of peace and comfort, reach out to a brother or sister in Christ. Be it the Lord Himself, or a brother or sister in Christ, reach out. God will take your worries from you, encourage and strengthen you, so cast off your burdens and unload yourself of your worries. Give it all up to God, then you will "have the peace that passes understanding down in your heart, where? down in your heart to staaay!"

Week V Notes

Week VI: Sharing Your Walk

Day One: Praying Together

Scriptures: Job 22:26-27; 2 Corinthians 1:10-11; Colossians 4:2-4

"When a Christian shuns fellowship with other Christians, the devil smiles. When he stops studying the Bible, the devil laughs. When he stops praying, the devil shouts for joy."
-- Corrie Ten Boom

Prayer is powerful. Prayer is important. Entire sermons have been preached on prayer and all its different aspects. On one occasion when Jesus was teaching his disciples, he told them, "Again, I tell you that if two of you on earth agree about anything you ask for, it will be done for you by my Father in heaven. For where two or three come together in my name, there am I with them" (Matthew 18:19-20). When two people are in agreement, our Father will do what we ask. Just two people praying together offer prayers powerful enough that our Father will do what they ask. Can you imagine if two hundred prayed? Two thousand???

Praying together in agreement brings Christians a tremendous advantage. We can and should use this to the advantage of the Kingdom, to further the cause of Christ's Kingdom. That is why we are directed to pray all throughout the Bible. Not only are we called to prayer in the Bible, but we are also shown how effective prayer can be. We are shown what it can accomplish.

Prayer is extremely effective, in all things, and when two of us pray in agreement, its effectiveness is a hundredfold. Great things can be accomplished by prayer and greater things when two or more pray together. Therefore we (that is, all Christians) need to be in agreement about prayer. We should pray with others. As you go through your day, see if you can not only pray for someone else, but see if you can pray *with* someone else.

Day Two: A Great Mission Tool

Scriptures: James 2:14-18

"Any ordinary favor we do for someone or any compassionate reaching out may seem to be going nowhere at first, but may be planting a seed we can't see right now. Sometimes we need to just do the best we can and then trust in an unfolding we can't design or ordain."
-- Sharon Salzberg

By providing for those in need who are not saved, you present a wonderful example of the Lord's love. After all wouldn't giving food to a hungry orphan or giving clothes to a man left out in the cold have more of an impact for God than preaching? For example, in the play Les Misérables, in the very beginning, Jean Valjean stole some silver from the church that had given him food and shelter. When the constable brought him back, the priest told him that the goods were not stolen but in fact a gift to Jean. That one event had such an impact on Jean that he completely changed his life. He went from being a hardened criminal to a very generous and giving man. The more successful he became in life, the more generous and giving he became. That one single event helped not only Jean Valjean, but many others through him.

In the same way, by giving to those in need, by providing for and assisting those who are without, we are having a great impact. It goes beyond the "talk the talk/walk the walk" expression. By taking an active interest in the needs of someone else, you are showing them God's Love first hand; you are filling God's promise to meet their needs. They, in turn, will likely go out and be inclined to help those individuals they see in need. When you give to those who are in need, to the unsaved in particular, you are doing more than just provided for their physical needs. You are providing for their spiritual need, their eternal security, as well. What's more your giving in that one situation could impact many other individuals as well. Is there someone you know who needs assistance? Why not see if you can show them God's love in a very practical way?

Day Three: Amazing Love

Scriptures: *1 John 4:10-12, Matthew 4:1-11, Luke 22:41-44*

"You give and give and give and still it's never enough. Your emotions have vanished that once held a thrill, you wonder if love could be alive in you still. But that ring on your finger was put there to stay, you'll never forget the words you promised that day. Jesus didn't die for you because it was fun, He hung there for love because it had to be done, and in spite of the anguish his word was fulfilled, cause love is not a feeling it's an act of your will."
-- Don Francisco

As I was driving home from a funeral not too long ago, I was listening to the radio and the song, "Amazing Love" began to play. It happens to be a favorite of mine, so I started singing along. The song came to the chorus when I was suddenly struck by just how true the words are. The line goes, *amazing love, how can it be that you my King would die for me.* Think about that. Jesus Christ our Lord and King gave up all the glory of Heaven to become a man. He got hungry, weary, tired, grief-stricken, and was overwhelmed with sorrow. Not only that, but he willingly gave up His life. Talk about love!

Jesus could have given up and given in at any time. He could have commanded stones to become bread when he was hungry. He could have called down twelve legions of angels to come rescue Him when He was being crucified. But He didn't. Jesus Christ endured it all. Our King died in our place to become our Savior. Our King willingly gave up His throne, and then willingly laid down His life so that we may live. Talk about Love!

When you realize just how much love our King has for us, it seems to just overflow inside you. With the amount of Love our Savior has for us, we should go out and pour His love on others. After all, how could we possibly keep it to ourselves? Nobody how has a light keeps it under a bushel. Nobody who is overflowing with God's great love for us should keep it to themselves. It was with Amazing Love that our King died for us, let us go out and pour out that same love on others.

Day Four: A Sacrifice of Praise

Scriptures: Hebrews 13:15-16

"It is easy to praise the Lord from the heights of His love, but it is rich to worship Him from the depths of His love. If you are in a time of testing or trial may I encourage you today to stop and worship the Lord. Find comfort in His word and in the obedience that comes from surrendering our will and rights to Him. Job prayed in the course of his trials, "Though He may slay me, I will hope in Him." Our Lord is sovereign - He is in control of all things. There is mercy in the wilderness dear friend. Come to Christ Jesus today, worship Him in spirit and truth, and drink of His mercy as He molds you to Himself."
-- Steve Camp, <u>Mercy in the Wilderness</u>

When Hurricane Katrina struck the gulf coast of the United States, my family and I lost everything we owned. I found a lot of solace in my Contemporary Christ CD's. Richard Mullins, in particular, had some great songs: *Hold Me Jesus* and *If I Stand* were wonderful.

Right after *If I Stand*, was the song, *Sing Your Praise to the Lord*. That was a much tougher song for me, given the circumstances. I needed to be held by Jesus, I was in no position to praise Him. Then that verse in Hebrews came to mind, "let us continually offer to God a sacrifice of praise." Notice it says "continually," not "when things are going right."

I believe a "sacrifice of praise" is just that: when praising God is a sacrifice. Sometimes it is easy to sing praises. Other times, it is not so easy. When you are in a position where you need to be held by Jesus and choose to praise Him instead, you are bringing a sacrifice of praise.

When we are together with our church family, or when things are going well for us, it is easy to praise God. However, when the chips are down, and we are alone, that is when praise becomes a sacrifice. It is also the most important time to praise Him. I drew strength from my savior through my sacrifice of praise. When you offer praise in spite of your circumstances instead of because them, you are offering up a sacrifice of praise and will draw your own strength from our Lord and Savior, Jesus Christ.

Day Five: Handling Adversity

Scriptures: Philippians 4:6-7, James 1:2-4

"We sometimes fear to bring our troubles to God, because they must seem small to Him who sitteth on the circle of the earth. But if they are large enough to vex and endanger our welfare, they are large enough to touch His heart of love. For love does not measure by a merchant's scales, not with a surveyor's chain. It hath a delicacy... unknown in any handling of material substance."
-- Reuben Archer (R. A.) Torrey

Many Atheists and other non-believers decry Christians saying "they use God as a crutch," or some other epithet to denote a dependence on Christ. Our reaction has been to shy away from this, try and hide it, try and seem bigger than we are. "Jesus is more than a crutch," we say. While that is true, he is everything to me, Jesus can in fact be just that a crutch. That seems so negative, doesn't it? A good part of that is due to the way non-believers use it in a derogatory way. A crutch. Can't operate without Christ. I may well catch flak for saying this but my response is, "Yep. So what?" So what if I run to God when the weight of the world seems unbearable. I am not ashamed to admit there are many points in my life I just would not have made it through had it not been for my Savior. There are plenty of times I need to use Christ as a "crutch."

I'll let you in on a little secret. While the world may look down upon you for needing the crutch of Christ, when you are actually going through adversity, they tend to admire the strength you have and the courage you show in the face of that adversity. By relying on Christ in your time of need, you are showing non-believers just what Jesus can, and does, do for us. He is there for us in our time of need. He saves us not only from our sins, but from the tribulations of life. That does not mean our lives will be a bed of roses. It means that when we hit hard times, we do not have to go at it alone. We have One we can lean on, One who is bigger than any problem we could ever face. If you are going through tough times, lean on your Savior. He will carry you though, and allow you to stand tall. Then those watching will know, crutch or not, Jesus is real and He helps those who need Him.

Day Six: Doing the Right Thing

Scripture: Hosea 10:12, Ephesians 6:10-15, Philippians 1:9-11

"Empower me to be a bold participant, rather than a timid saint in waiting; to exercise authority of honesty, rather than to defer to power or deceive to get it; to influence someone for justice, rather than impress anyone for gain; and by grace, to find treasures of joy, of friendship, of peace hidden in the fields you give me daily to plow."
-- Ted Loder

What is righteousness? The Amplified Bible gives us a little bit of a clue in its rendering of Ephesians 6:14: "...having put on the breastplate of integrity and of moral rectitude and right standing with God..." Integrity, moral rectitude and right standing with God. When most people think of righteousness, they think of right standing with God. However, what about integrity? Integrity can best be defined as doing the right thing when nobody is watching. It could be as simple as stopping at a stop sign in the middle of the night when no one is around, or returning extra change you may have received to the cashier. When I was in school, my first year was known as "plebe year." As plebes, there were many crazy rules we needed to follow to help build our discipline and commitment. One of these was walking six inches from the walls of the passageways at all times.

After a while, it became habit, but at first it was rather unusual, and even a pain in the neck sometimes. Another rule we had was no talking in the passageways. Both were easier to break then they were to follow, but the punishments could be severe. Underneath our barracks was a connecting passageway called "o-deck". There were lots of corners and turns, plenty of places where "nobody was watching." It would have been real easy to cut a corner by leaving the six inch limit, or talk to a friend, with nobody ever finding out. For the most part, my classmates and I did do the right thing, even though it would have been real easy to break the rules and "get away with it." None of us were perfect, but the Bible does not ask us for perfection, rather integrity, and if you can do the right thing even when it would be easy to do the wrong one, even when you will definitely not get caught, doing the right thing takes and shows integrity.

Day Seven: Whacking Moles

Scripture: Luke 12:22-32

"We often think of great faith as something that happens spontaneously so that we can be used for a miracle or healing. However, the greatest faith of all, and the most effective, is to live day by day trusting Him. It is trusting Him so much that we look at every problem as an opportunity to see His work in our life. It is not worrying, but rather trusting and abiding in the peace of God that will crush anything that Satan tries to do to us. If the Lord created the world out of chaos, He can easily deal with any problem that we have."
-- Rick Joyner

When I was a little kid, there was a popular game at the arcade called "Wak'a'mole." You took this big plastic hammer, and watched as little moles would pop up from any one of about 9 or 12 different holes. The more moles you "whacked," the more points you got.

The thing is, no matter how many times you whacked a particular mole, it kept coming up, and no sooner did you whack one mole than another would pop up. If that were not enough, the more you whacked, the faster they popped up! After a short while of whacking moles, things would get pretty complicated. Sometimes I feel like my life is a game of "wak'a'mole."

Problems just seem to pop up. Sometimes over and over again, and no sooner do I get one problem solved then another "pops" right up again. To top it all off, the more I solve problems the faster they seem to come! Life itself can get pretty complicated, and sometimes, overwhelming.

Fortunately, I have a Father in Heaven who is bigger than any problem I could ever have. When they seem to pop up, I simply run to Him, tell Him the problem, and let Him take care of it for me. He has never failed me. Every problem I bring to Him gets solved. If your "moles" are overwhelming you, why not go to your Father in Heaven? He is sitting there with a plastic hammer waiting to whack it for you!

Week VI Notes

Week VII: Walking With the Body

Day One: Accepting In Love

Scriptures: Romans 14:1-8

"Loving-kindness and compassion are the basis for wise, powerful, sometimes gentle, and sometimes fierce actions that can really make a difference -- in our own lives and those of others."
-- Sharon Salzberg

I'll be the first to admit it: I am not a lovable person. Some who know me may disagree with that statement, but those who know me well would most certainly agree. The thing is, in spite of all my faults, the people who know me well like me anyway. They accept me as I am, warts and all.

Who is the person who knows you the best? Think about how well they know you. They know all your deepest secrets; they know all your faults. They know every stinkin' thing about you, and yet, they love you anyway. They accept you, just as you are.

Now imagine someone who knows you even better then the person who knows you the best. Someone who knows every detail of your life. Every skeleton, every dark deed is visible, and yet, He loves you. He loves you more than any one has ever loved in the history of love.

This is our Father in Heaven. He knows our deepest, darkest secrets. The dirt we never share with anyone is right before His eyes, and He loves us! The Bible tells us, "God demonstrates his own love for us in this: While we were still sinners, Christ died for us." God sent His only Son to die for us... and He did so while we were sinners, but more, He did so *because* we were sinners. Talk about love!

There is nothing we can hide from God, but there is nothing that we need to hide from Him. Sure, we may be ashamed, and rightly so, but our Heavenly Father sees all that we are ashamed of and loves us anyway! He washes away our dirt with the blood of Jesus Christ and allows us to walk in His Grace. Oh, how He loves us so! Let us show that same love to our brothers and sisters in Christ.

Day Two: Jesus' Wife

Scriptures: 1 Cor. 3:18-20, James 1:5-6, 3:13-17

"Jesus is life
The air I'm breathing
Why my heart is beating
Everything I'm needing
Jesus is life!"
-- Steven Curtis Chapman

Steven Curtis Chapman has a song called "Jesus is Life." When my daughter was little, this song was a favorite of hers. Only what Mr. Chapman sang and what my daughter heard were not exactly the same thing. See, my daughter though he was singing Jesus' wife. I can remember the first time I heard her. We were on a road trip, a mix CD was in the stereo, and this song came on. She sang along from the beginning and when the chorus came on, she sang along as loud as she could, "JESUS' WIFE!" It was hard not to laugh.

Too many times what we say is not what is heard by others. We may think we are clearly communicating our ideas, only to have somebody misunderstand what it is we are trying to say. Quite often, people repeat what they think they heard instead of what was actually said, and often as loud as they can. One of the biggest causes of dissension in the ranks, aside from pride, is simply miscommunication. This happens in all forms of communication. What could often be clarified with a quick explanation instead becomes a source of dissension. Is there something you heard or read that does not seem right? Think one of you brothers and sisters has said something strange or "off?" Why not ask what they meant first? Take a moment and learn what your brother and sister are truly saying.

If we can take the time to seek clarification and work to clear up any possible misunderstandings before they occur, we would go a long way to laying aside our differences. Then, instead of fighting over differences that do not truly exist, we can work together with one purpose and praise God with one voice.

Day Three: As I Have Loved You

Scriptures: John 13:33-34

"Your task is not to seek for love, but merely to seek and find all the barriers within yourself that you have built against it."
-- Rumi

Christians are their own worst enemy. Madalyn Murray O'Hair is credited with saying, "The army of the Lord is the only army that shoots its wounded." This statement is all too true. Far be it from me to agree with a lady who made it her life's mission to completely remove God from the public sphere, but the sad truth is, what she said is correct. Jesus told us that the world would know we are His by the love we show each other, and yet the love of God is often missing from our groups. Instead we often see some of most hurtful, mean spirited comments directed towards each other. Why? Because of a disagreement in doctrine or worse, a perceived slight. The phrase "turn the other cheek" is lost as Christians tend to be the most vindictive assemblage of people.

The sad thing is, not only have I seen it with my own eyes and experience it first hand, I have said things with my own lips and typed them with my own hands. I have been on both sides of the anger and bitterness. It shames me to admit it, but I have caused quite a bit of pain to my fellow brothers and sisters. I would be willing to wager that anybody reading this has done the same. Thus, I propose a pledge. I will vow before each and every one of you that I will refrain from treating my family in Christ with antagonism. I will instead show them love and turn the other cheek when need be. I will be understanding of their different opinions and I will not respond in kind when assaulted verbally.

Will you join me in this pledge?

Day Four: United We Stand, Divided We Fall

Scriptures: Ephesians 4:2-6

"For too long, we have focused on our differences - in our politics and backgrounds, in our race and beliefs - rather than cherishing the unity and pride that binds us together."
-- Bob Riley

United we stand, divided we fall. Right now Christ's Church is divided, and we are falling fast. Only by being united can we stand. If we can be united in Christ, then we can stand firm on the truth. Christianity is under a fierce onslaught, not just in America, but all over the world. Instead of fighting each other, Christians need to start supporting each other. When the world tries to make the Federal Courts establish Atheism as the national religion, we should call them on it.

If we are fighting each other, we will not have the time or the resources, nor will anyone pay heed to what we are saying. Our infighting discredits us in the eyes of the world. The enemy is using our own weapons against us, and we are too busy fighting each other to notice! The world considers us hypocrites as we preach love and viciously fight one another. We need to stop. We cannot carry on as we have been. We need to be examples of Christ's love. We need to show that love to each other and to the world. We need to be one in our Savior.

We need to start praying. We need to pray together. Only by standing and praying together do we have a chance at stopping the massed assault launched against us. Only by relying on the Lord Jesus Christ do we have a chance at overcoming the world. Only united will we stand. Only when we unite in Christ, will we be able to stand firm on the Truth, defend the faith, win souls and further the kingdom of Jesus Christ, our Lord!

Day Five: Freedom!

Scriptures: Galatians 5:1, 13-14

"The moment we choose to love we begin to move against domination, against oppression. The moment we choose to love we begin to move towards freedom, to act in ways that liberate ourselves and others. That action is the testimony of love as the practice of freedom."
-- Bell Hooks

If you have seen Braveheart, you know the ending is both sad and encouraging. After a day of horrid torture, William Wallace is near death. With his last breath of life, he lets out a shout that stuns friends and enemies alike: "FREEEEEDDOOOOMMM!!"

Every July 4th, Americans celebrate their freedom, given to us 243[1] years ago, but a courageous group of men who risked death themselves, for defying the same crown... the King of England. 243[1] years ago, delegates from 13 colonies declared their freedom from tyranny by signing the Declaration of Independence, one of the most sacred documents in U.S. History. It was penned by Thomas Jefferson, and hotly debated for two solid days. Then, in the hot meeting hall in Philadelphia, the delegates affixed their signatures to the document that would become the foundation of a revolution.

As Christians, we have another reason to celebrate: Our Freedom in Christ. Through Christ, we are freed from the bondage of sin and death. Does this mean we go on sinning, and take advantage of our freedom? "By no means!" (Rom 6:1). With freedom comes responsibility. We are freed from the wages of sin, but we must use that freedom to 1) walk in the Light and 2) help set others free.

[1]As of 2019, when 3rd Edition was prepared (TRU)

Day Six: Acceptance

Scripture: Romans 15:5-8

"Perhaps the most important thing we bring to another person is the silence in us, not the sort of silence that is filled with unspoken criticism or hard withdrawal. The sort of silence that is a place of refuge, of rest, of acceptance of someone as they are."
-- Rachel Naomi Remen

When my family and I first moved back to the states, we started looking around for a church to attend. We found one that suited us and I decided to meet with the pastor. For our first meeting I was going to put my best foot forward. Everyone wants to make a good first impression on the pastor, right?

I had thought very carefully ahead of time how I would steer the conversation, to paint myself is a good light, yet, when we met, I wound up doing the exact opposite! Every flaw, every bit of dirt came out onto the table. I was fully exposed. I remember, when I left I thought, "man, he is *never* going to want to talk to me again!" Much to my surprise, however, he did. We met quite frequently and became good friends.

My pastor learned every bad thing about me upfront. The first impression I gave him was not a good one, but he accepted me. Regardless of the mistakes I had made, the bad judgments, the skeletons in my closet, that pastor accepted me, just as I was.

Would that all Christians were that way! Can you imagine how effective we would be for Christ if we accepted one another, regardless of how different we are or how bad our pasts may be? If Christians would love each other regardless of the mistakes, bad judgments or skeletons in all our closets, the church would be a force to be reckoned with!

Why not make an effort to accept your brothers and sisters in Christ, regardless of their differences from you, just as Christ accepted you.

Day Seven: Moving Mountains

Scripture: Matthew 17:14-21, Hebrews 11:1-3

"Faith is also a plea for the everlasting light, a thirst for this illumination and transfiguration. This light continues to shine, through the darkness and evil, through the drab grayness and dull routine of this world, like a ray of sun piercing through the clouds. It is recognized by the soul, it comforts the heart, it makes us feel alive, and it transfigures us from within."
-- Alexander Schmemann

Faith really can move mountains. Jesus said so. When his disciples asked him to increase their faith he responded, "I tell you the truth, if you have faith as small as a mustard seed, you can say to this mountain, 'Move from here to there' and it will move. Nothing will be impossible for you" (Matt 17:20). Jesus uses the mustard seed as an example for a reason: they are very tiny. He's saying quite clearly just a tiny bit of faith is enough.

That small amount is enough to move mountains. Many times our problems can seem quite 'mountainous.' Just like physical mountains, all we need is a tiny bit of faith to tell them to move, and they will. While you are in the midst of these problems, it is very easy to lose sight of that. It can be hard to see the solution when the problem is overshadowing, but that is ok.

We do not need to be faith giants to overcome; all we need is the amount of one little mustard seed. Jesus will take the little bit of faith we offer, along with our problems, and take care of us. No problem is too great, nor is any trouble too small. The Bible is full of examples of just that: Abraham, Caleb, David, even Job. While some of them went on to become "giants of faith," none of them started out that way.

Each of them took their own mustard seed sized amount of faith and trust God with their problems. God took that little bit of faith and carried them through. God will carry you thought, as well. Turn your problems over to Him. Trust Him with just minute amount of faith and you will see your problems move right out of your way.

Week VII Notes

Week VIII: Standing on the Rock

Day One: What Are You Building On?

Scriptures: Matthew 7:24-27

"Adversity is like a strong wind. It tears away from us all but the things that cannot be torn, so that we see ourselves as we really are."
-- Arthur Golden

One morning, while driving into work I was listening to the radio and the news talked about the flooding in the northeast. The rains had stopped and the floodwaters have started to recede. I was reminded of Jesus' parable about the two builders. One build his house on sand and one built his house on rock. When the rains came, the flood waters washed away the house build on sand, but the house built on the rock stood firm.

The governor of Rhode Island said they have not seen that much rain or flooding in hundred years. One hundred years. That's a long time! The people probably were not expecting the rain or flooding to get to such a level. Back in 2005, I thought my house was secure. I looked at the elevation maps and the flood plain maps and my house was in a good spot. It was secure. We were secure. Two months later, Katrina proved me wrong. The waters reached a level of four feet in my "secure" house, ruining everything inside.

Quite often, we feel our spiritual houses are secure. We look at our finances and see a sizable savings. We are indispensible at work and know our job is safe. We are in perfect health, eat right and exercise regularly. Quite often, when the spiritual hurricanes come our way, we are proven wrong. There is only one way our spiritual houses can be secure, and that is when they are firmly grounded in the rock, Jesus Christ. Finances, savings, jobs, even health are all fleeting, but Jesus Christ is eternal and never changing. When your house is built upon him, no storm or hurricane can ruin it. What is your house built on?

Day Two: Lessons From Unbelievers

Scriptures: John 13:31-35

"The most important thing in life is to learn how to give out love, and to let it come in."
-- Morrie Schwartz

One particular summer, during the a period of Annual Training with the National Guard unit I was a member of at that time, I became good friends with two of my peers. One is Hindu and the other is an atheist. The atheist was actually my roommate for part of the time I was there, and many interesting discussions were had between us. The thing that interested me most, however, was not the discussions we had, but the *actions* of my friends. Not only were they very open about their beliefs and very patient in explaining things to me, but they are two of the nicest people I know. They were very quick to provide ample help in many different areas. They were so helpful that I inadvertently offended/hurt one of them when I declined an offer to borrow a vehicle for the time I was there.

The Bible tells us that we are love each other, support each other and help each other. There are many Christians who live up to what the Bible says. However, I would venture to say that many do not, at least not in the way they should. I know fall short more than I care to admit, and yet here are two people, who do not believe in Jesus, who lived up to His words better than most of His followers.

Please understand that I am not trying to say that one group of beliefs is better than another, but rather show how the actions of these two, good friends have caused me to look deep within myself. How often do I show love to my neighbor? How many times have I helped people when I've been in the position to do so? Some may be offended, others may see the irony, in that I am striving to live more like Jesus based on the actions of somebody who does not believe in Him. Regardless, I have learned that one can be surprised at just how far a little bit of love can go.

Day Three: Never Forget

Scriptures: Joshua 1:5-9

"Never forget that God is your friend. And like all friends, He longs to hear what's been happening in your life. Good or bad, whether it's been full of sorrow or anger, or even when you're questioning why terrible things have to happen."
-- Nicholas Sparks (The Last Song)

I remember exactly where I was when the planes struck on 9-11. I was sitting down to dinner in the forward wardroom on the USS CARL VINSON. Yes, you read that right, I was sitting down to dinner. I was in the middle of the Arabian Sea and we had just done the hand off with the ENTERPRISE battle group. One of the fighter pilots mentioned that a plane had struck one of the towers.

I saw the second plane hit. Actually, I saw the explosion that resulted when the second plane hit. I also saw the first planes launch and the first tomahawk missiles fly towards their targets in Afghanistan. A few days after Operation Enduring Freedom began, Gordon England, then Secretary of the Navy, came out to visit the battle group. I do not remember much of his speech, but there was one thing he said that stuck with me. He told us that when President George Bush had his first meeting with the National Security Council, he looked every one of them in the eye and said, "Never forget." Mr. England then looked at us and said, "Never forget."

As Christians, it can be too easy to forget God. It can be too easy to forget that He is the middle of our tragedies. It can be too easy to forget that He is in control. However, on 9-11, God was there. He was in control, providing courage to the responders, strength the victims and comfort to their families.

When you go through the storms of your life, when you are so overcome with grief or fear, never forget that God is with you each and every step of the way.

Day Four: God of Grace

Scriptures: Psalm 51:15-17

God of grace and God of glory,   *Save us from weak resignation,*
On Thy people pour Thy power.   *To the evils we deplore.*
Crown Thine ancient church's story, *Let the search for Thy salvation,*
Bring her bud to glorious flower.   *Be our glory evermore.*
Grant us wisdom, grant us courage, *Grant us wisdom, grant us courage,*
For the facing of this hour.   *Serving Thee Whom we adore.*
    -- Harry E. Fosdick, *God of Grace God of Glory*

I used to joke with friends that if God had a "last ever-lovin' nerve" that I was on it. Soon however it became no joke. Like Paul, I yearn to serve our Father in Heaven. Yet my flesh pulls me in the exact opposite direction. As time goes on, it gets easier to follow the desires of the spirit and ignore the desires of the flesh, but I still fall. Still, I refrain from doing what the Lord wants to do... or worse, I do it grudgingly. Sometimes it feels like I am doomed!

I am NOT doomed, however. When I fall, God picks me up, dusts me off and sets me on His path. Sometimes He is gentle, but sometimes He is not. The Bible tells us, "not [to] lose heart when he rebukes you, because the Lord disciplines those he loves, and he punishes everyone he accepts as a son" (Hebrews 12:5b-6). Sometimes that requires complete brokenness on our part.

In order to be used by God, we need to be molded by God. That often entails a breaking down of self... a breaking down of our flesh and sinful desires, so we can be raised in spirit by the Grace of God. We are sinful creatures. Like Paul, I often feel like the chief of sinners. Like Paul I ask, "Who will rescue me from this body of death?" (Romans 7:24) Like Paul, I answer, "Thanks be to God—through Jesus Christ our Lord!" (v. 25).

Through the sacrifice of our Lord and Savior, Jesus Christ, God extends His grace to us, not so that we can go on sinning (Romans 6:1-2), but so that we can turn away from our sins and follow Him! We can serve God because of His great love and His immense grace. Yes, like Paul, I will answer: "Thanks be to God—through Jesus Christ our Lord!"

Day Five: Our God is a God of Second Chances

Scriptures: Philippians 4:6-7, James 1:2-4

> *Praise the Lord!*
> *He's the God of second chances!*
> *You'll be floored how His love your life enhances!*
> *You can be restored from your darkest circumstances!*
> *Our God is a God of second chances!*
>   *-- Jonah: A Veggie Tales Adventure*

Not too long ago, my church did mission in the inner city. I felt called by God to go and participate in this event. The tug was pretty strong. However, it was something I really did not want to do. The excuses were not in short supply: it was hot, I don't have any supplies, I'm no good at that sort of thing, on and on ad naseaum. Still, I felt as if God *really* wanted me to do this. The excuses won out.

That's right. In spite of the pull on my spirit, I sat that one out. Like Jonah, God gave me an assignment and I went the opposite direction. There were no storms at sea, nor was I swallowed by a whale, but I did notice a change in my walk with God. It was not a change for the better, either. Life itself became much more stressful, at least it seems that way.

Please understand, it was not the mission that was necessarily the key, but the fact that I had deliberately disobeyed God...simply because I didn't want to do what He told me to. I am truly ashamed. I had no good reason, I just didn't want to. Like Jonah, I humbled myself before God and asked for his forgiveness. God was gracious and merciful. He not only forgave me, He gave me another assignment! This time, I was quick to obey. It was not easy either. It cost me a lot of time and really wore me down...to the point where I had to call in sick for work! Still, God gave me a second chance! He forgave me and restored me. The turnaround was immediate and tangible. My walk was better, even everyday life became less stressful and more manageable.

Obeying God was hard, but disobeying Him made things so much harder. It is hard to go through your day when you are not right with God. Fortunately for us, our God is a God of second chances!

Day Six: What's in Your Bible?

Scripture: 2 Timothy 3:15-18

"All intimacy is rare -- that's what makes it precious. And it involves the revelation of one's self and the loving gaze upon another's true self. Intimacy requires honesty and kindness in almost equal measure, trust and trustworthiness, forgiveness and the capacity to be forgiven . . . It's more than worth it."
-- Amy Bloom

I love marking up my bible. Some people like to keep their Bible pristine, some like to mark it up. I am a marker. I underline, highlight, star, box, circle, you name it, I've done it. It helps me when I am studying passages again and again. Eventually though, the Bible itself gets so worn that it needs to be replaced.

This happened to me after Hurricane Katrina. My Bible had been with me since my high school graduation and had been all over the world with me. When we evacuated for the hurricane it was one of the "essentials" that I grabbed and thus one of our few surviving items. Alas, it was in rough shape by that point. After well over a decade of use and having been dragged all over the world, the binding was shot. Big chunks of the concordance had fallen out. More pages were loose. I tried tape, but that was just a short term solution.

Eventually, I needed to face the hard truth: It was time to replace my Bible. While part of me was sad to let the old one go, part of me was also excited. There is something about breaking in a new Bible. Reading the passages fresh once more. Gleaning new things from passages that you poured over and marked up. To help ensure that I would be looking at things fresh, I refrained from copying my notes and underlines, etc.

The result was great! I had a fresh Bible ready for the marking! Do you mark up your Bible? Do you use it enough that it needs to be replaced? Ask yourself, What's in my Bible?

Day Seven: Remember

Scripture: Psalm 91:5-16

"Every goal, every action, every thought, every feeling one experiences, whether it be consciously or unconsciously known, is an attempt to increase one's level of peace of mind."
-- Sydney Madwed

When I replaced my worn and torn Bible I started with a clean slate, but there was one exception. Right above Psalm 91 was the word, "Remember." I wrote this word after Katrina, and wanted to make sure the memory would last with my new Bible. See, when it comes to spiritual lessons, I have a very short memory. I am not proud of this fact, but it is, well, a fact. I found that when I went through any sort of trial, I was learning the same lessons, over and over and over... and over.

This time, I was determined to learn the lesson and take it to heart, so I wrote the word "Remember" over Psalm 91. Every day, I read that psalm and I remember how God brought me through each and every trial I faced after the hurricane hit. It was not just the loss of our home and all our worldly goods. It was dealing with the fallout. Working with my creditors after the storm hit and again after I had lost my job. Trying to get the insurance company to pay up, trying to get the mortgage company to accept the money and finally, the betrayal of a close Christian companion.

Katrina was not just the most damaging storm in terms of property loss. For me, it was the most damaging spiritual storm I have ever faced. I was quite damaged, and still am in some respects. However, through it all, God was with me and to this day, I will remember everything He did for me. To this day, when I read Psalm 91, I will remember the lessons I learned. To this day, I will remember.

Week VIII Notes

www.ingramcontent.com/pod-product-compliance
Lightning Source LLC
Chambersburg PA
CBHW060121050426
42448CB00010B/1980